THE WANDERER

WRITTEN BY
P.E.HARRIS

ILLUSTRATED BY
RUXANDRA ȘERBĂNOIU

Teachable Moment Series

Introduction

Writing 'The Wanderer' was the most fun I've had writing a children's book. Living in several different countries and visiting many more has helped mold a more universal perspective that I hope will be visible in the writing. Hopefully you will enjoy not only the new direction of the poems, but the new illustrations as well. Thanks again for your support!

Table of Contents

Breakfast

What is this strange concoction,
That my mother makes me eat?
It's not a fruit! Doesn't taste like bread!
And it's def'nitely not meat!

It's pasty, thick and strange to see!
Unlike anything I've known!
Is this what it means to be grown up?
I had hoped for tea and scones!

It's not that bad! I think I like!
One spoon's turned into ten!
This oatmeal stuff is pretty good!
I think I'll eat again!

1

Celestial

The Sun and the Moon had a contest,
To see who could shine the most light!
And even though they were friends, and would be 'til the end,
They both fashioned themselves as bright!

And though it would seem, that the Sun's radiant beams,
Could win without breaking a sweat,
The moon hedged his bet, so he never did fret,
As he cooly enacted his scheme!

He convinced all the birds, insects, beasts, even men,
That his light was the strongest there was!
He put on an act, all while stating as fact,
That which wasn't true, simply 'cause!

He told them grand stories of vic'tries and trials,
Of battles he'd won, foes he'd beat!
He'd lavish his tales, all while casting a veil,
On the Sun and his im'nent defeat!

On the day of the contest, the table was set,
Contestants both eager to see,
How the cosmos, the people, and the stars would all judge,
This battle for supremacy!

The birds, beasts and stars, all sang the Sun's praise,
But it wasn't enough, for you see...
The men were the loudest, and thought they were right,
'Cause they fell for the Moon's fallacy!

The Sun was defeated, at least history says,
And the Moon's victory through ages was told,
But the Sun is still shining, and always will be,
Because truth always favors the bold!

Dentist Visit

Today's my dentist trip, you see!
It happens twice per year.
I can't say that I'm happy though -
In fact I'm filled with fear!

They poke and prod, they scrape and drill,
They rinse and then repeat!
It's like I'm trapped within a cage,
Of fear, pain and defeat!

But truthfully it's not that bad,
Once I get past despair!
She's gentle when she cleans my teeth,
It's painless 'cause she cares!

She takes her time and does it right,
And leaves me feeling new!
She makes me thankful for my teeth,
And grateful when I chew!

Flags

Flags are interesting to me, because they give a glimpse -
Into a country's history - It seems so 'common sense.'

But what is common sense to you may not be that to me -
So I'll take the time to listen/learn, and through your eyes
I'll see -

A new perspective- a new way to think - a new path by
which to walk -
A chance to understand the 'why' and not complain or balk -

At a life that may be different from the one I know and
see,
But nonetheless reflects their truth, their life, and what
they've seen.

So take the time to listen to the ones from 'round the world,
And understand their 'common sense' when their flags are then
unfurled.

Fred

Fred the lime green brontosaurus,
Loves to read his big thesaurus,
Then go play with Stegosaurus,
Hide and seek with Tyrannosaurus,
Snack on fungi (polyporus),
Dine on big ferns (cyclosorus),
Then stare at constellations (Taurus),
While singing in the bronto-chorus!

Fun In The Sun

Fifteen waddling, quacking ducks,
Went down to the pond for a swim!
When along came a goose, a hedgehog and a moose,
And joined along with their walk on a whim!

They swam and they played, danced and idled away,
Their day in the sun in the pond!
New friendships were made, as they danced in the glade,
With their new common interest their bond!

Government Sheep

When it's time to sleep, I prop up my feet,
And dream of government sheep!

They neigh and bleat, they run and leap,
These darn government sheep!

They never seem to lead or read,
These strange government sheep!

They only want to play and feed,
These starved government sheep!

Tonight I'll count sleep-goats instead,
Of these useless government sheep,

And tomorrow I'll wake up refreshed,
'Cause the sheep made not a peep!

Growing Up

What shall I be when I grow up?
A fireman or a priest?
Maybe a court reporter,
Or a caterer of feasts!

Maybe a welder to build the world!
Maybe a teacher too!
I guess I could do all those things,
Or at least just one or two!

Joys of Reading

There's a certain joy in reading,
It compares to nothing else!
You can lose yourself in far-off lands,
Just take a book from off the shelf!

Imagination runs wild and free,
As you smile at every turn,
When you're finished, though you're sad it's done,
The desire to read still burns!

Jungle Jags

South of the equator,
In beautiful Peru,
There lived three jaguar brothers,
Whose spots were green and blue!

They roamed the jungles, high and low,
Always searching for a meal,
But along the way, they laughed and played,
And repped their jungle life with zeal!

These jaguars were unique you see,
Not just in their pretty spots!
Only eating fruits and vegetables,
So their food was never 'caught'

Lucuma, Chirimoya, and Dragon Fruits,
Were their favorite fruits by far!
Cocona, Tumbo, and Aguaje,
Made their diets seem bizarre!

But because their spots made them stand out,
And they could not hunt or stalk,
They decided that it's just as well,
So now instead of run, they walk!

They take each day just as it comes,
Always adapting to the change!
And live their jungle lives with joy,
Never seeing themselves as strange!

Little Runaway

I think I'll run away today -
My parents make me mad!
They make me go to bed at 9:00,
My friends all think that's sad!

I've packed some rollups and string cheese,
Hot Pockets and Hi-C!
My mobile phone is fully charged,
In case someone needs me!

I've made it now! I've walked three blocks!
I feel I'm finally free!
No more early bedtime mess!
No parents to boss me!

I'm getting hungry and it's getting hot!
But I can't find a microwave!
My drink is warm and my food is cold,
Guess I'll just eat it in the shade.

It's hotter now and I've walked ten blocks,
My mom will be calling soon!
I think they've learned their lesson now,
So I'll be back home at noon!

No Nose

I thought I'd blow my nose today,
Because I had to sneeze you see!
But I didn't think it through, I guess -
I used too much velocity!

I wonder if my nose is there!
I knew I blew too hard!
I'm sure it's gone! Oh no! It is!
I've lost it in the yard!

Open Eyes

There once was an invisible girl,
She didn't fit in, you see!
It wasn't that she could not be seen,
People just didn't bother to see!

She walked each day to school and back,
Alone and a little sad,
That she couldn't make friends with the popular kids,
Or dress up in the latest fads!

She played catch by herself in the yard at recess,
While the other kids played on fun teams!
She had lunch at a table reserved just for one,
Where she ate ham and cheese, still unseen.

'Til one day a teacher of science and fact,
Spotted her all alone as she walked,
The young teacher approached, but tried not to encroach,
Then slowly she smiled as they talked!

It seemed as though Amy (Invisible Girl),
Had a new friend with eyes that could see!
Their relationship grew, because finally she knew,
It was her job to see, not be seen!

Purple Butterfly

I saw a purple butterfly,
And she landed on my hand!
She looked at me, as though she'd seen,
My face before, and then...

She flew in circles, long and slow,
As I watched with childish glee!
Up then down, then side to side,
As she danced mid-air, then she...

Stopped for just a second,
And lit upon my nose!
Then I swear, she smiled and said,
"I'm with you 'cause you chose...

To see me as a pretty thing,
Not unusual or strange!
You embraced my unique countenance,
Without pause or hate or shame!"

I learned a lesson, that fine day!
Never judge by how one looks!
A man in orange may be a saint,
And a suited one, a crook!

So treat each other with respect!
You'll be surprised at what you see!
Assume the best in those you meet,
A purple butterfly they may be!

Questions

I have tons of questions, like what will I do today?
What will I eat? What will I drink? What will I wear to play?

Where'd I come from? Where will I go? When will I learn
to read?
What do I like? What do I want? What do I really need?

Who do I love? And who loves me? Who else knows that I'm
here?
I'm just swingin' in my baby crib, and grinnin' ear to ear!

Rainbows

There's a rainbow in the distance!
It's colors, blue and green,
With yellows, reds, and oranges too,
And royal abergine!

I heard that it's a prism,
Nothing more and nothing less,
But there's something there I can't perceive,
And I'm confused, I must confess!

What of its stately nature?
So distinct and picturesque!
They seem to show up after floods,
To bring beauty to the mess!

I guess I'll go on wondering -
Searching its bands for clues!
But guess what - I don't have to know!
To keep questioning, I choose!

Reflecting Forest

Lightning-fast turtles, molasses-slow rabbits,
And bears that can talk while they read,

Creeks that run upstream, and trees that grow down,
But fall upwards, their leaves, nuts and seeds!

A stunning display of blue grass and green skies,
Against backdrops of silver and gold!

In this place you can see, a changed version of me,
One that's loving and trusting and bold!

Roasted Chicken

I love to eat roasted chicken!
I have to eat it every day!
This started just one year ago,
So now I've got to find a way,

To curb this needful craving,
This untamed, robust need!
This urgency to feed my greed -
My tummy must be freed,

To eat some beef stew, fish and corn,
Tomatoes, cukes and kale,
Carrots, chives and celery,
A steak, salmon or quail!

At this point I will eat anything,
My situation's dire!
Seaweed chips or century eggs,
Greasy twinkies from a fryer!

Alligator on a stick,
A scorpion on a grill!
A porcupine that's soaked in brine,
Even if it still has quills!

But then again, when I think of it,
This chicken's pretty good!
It sure beats eating porcupine -
They taste like dirt and wood!

The Wanderer

I decided to go wandering,
So I set off across town!
And as I neared the mirror shop,
A voice told me "slow down!"

And as I peered into the shop,
I peered into myself,
And learned to love what the world could see -
In a mirror on a shelf!

Timmy the Tadpole

Timmy the Tadpole,
Enjoys tuna casserole,
While watching cartoons on TV!

He'd frequently question,
His painful digestion,
Then blame it on tuna, you see!

Truth

There's no such thing as multitasking,
No good job done without asking,
Questions and queries for clarity,
First-time perfection's a rarity!

We fall, we rise, and we find a way,
As long as we learn, we win the day!
So stand up, be seen, learn from your past,
And you'll find your strength and truth at last!

Universal Truth

There is balance in the Universe -
A rhythm to the rhyme!
A cadence in a perfect dance,
That transcends space and time!

It flows through me, and flows through you!
It flows with perfect grace!
It flows through rocks and flows through trees,
And stands in justice's place!

It recognizes motives -
The pure ones taking stage,
As recipients of blessings,
Are bestowed with wisdom sage!

Wild Horses

Wild horses roamed the Texas plains,
Under the wide, blue skies.
They ate fresh sage and drank from streams,
The wind and birds, allies!

They frolicked and ran fast and free,
'Til we fenced the untamed plains!
Now they work our farms and run our tracks,
And they eat their corn and grains!

Wind Chimes

I find wind chimes relaxing,
They play such soothing songs!
And each one is a melody,
Some short and some are long!

Each and every song's unique -
It is never heard again!
And it gives the gift of music,
To the wayward, drifting wind!

Zoo Paradox

My Mom surprised me yesterday,
With two tickets to the zoo,
But I've got mixed feelings now you see,
Cause the animals make me blue!

To see them caged and so restrained,
Makes me feel a twinge of guilt.
I feel as though they're in a show,
One that on their backs was built.

But my mom is so excited,
It's as if she just can't see,
My troubling zoo dilema -
And the paradox in me

About the Author

Thanks for reading! If you enjoyed this book or found it useful I'd be very grateful if you'd post a short review on Amazon. Your support really does make a difference and I read all reviews personally.

Thanks again for your support!

P.E. Harris

Other book titles by P.E. Harris

Made in the USA
Columbia, SC
01 November 2022

70321286R00024